Walking Along the Ice Age Trail

ANNETTE TOWLER

Walking Along The Ice Age Trail

Copyright © 2021 by Annette Towler

All rights reserved

Published by Red Penguin Books

Bellerose Village, New York

ISBN

Print 978-1-63777-209-6

Digital 978-1-63777-208-9

No part of this book may be reproduced in any form or by any electronic or mechanical means, including information storage and retrieval systems, without written permission from the author, except for the use of brief quotations in a book review.

Contents

Walking Along the Ice Age Trail	1
Neigh to Necrophilia	3
Flowing with Fartlek along Lake Michigan	5
Leap into the Lake	7
Looking Out from Lookout Mountain	9
Lily White	11
Women of Afghanistan	13
Toasty with Triage	15
Away To Provence	17
Pandemic Periodontal	19
Echo Ecstasy	21
Elegy for living	23
Take You Home	25
Marathon Blues	27
The Difficult Ones	29
Kiss For a Therapist	31
Education For Americans	33
A picture of us	37
About the Author	39

Walking Along the Ice Age Trail

Walking along the Ice Age Trail

With You

Our footsteps sink into the ancient soil

The two of us without any of the crowds bursting their lungs

At a million decibels, quiet are we

Pondering which way to turn and I tell you that the place reminds me of England

The England that I remember when my mother wore a scarf of blue to cover the rollers

Our laughter is quiet as we consider what it means to be human and middle-aged

Facing our own mortality on the Ice Age Trail

Your presence is a quiet rapture, every nerve within me settled

You tell me that you like it when I let my hair down because my face is slim

I tell you that you look like a boy

And we are children again, innocent in our steps seeking rest and recovery

After many years of work, both of us with our awards to show the toil

I look into your eyes, so brown that I sink into the soil on the Ice Age Trail

My hand, your hand snug inside the lines of years, resting and recuperating

Glad for peace, walking along a path brimming with promise of the twilight years.

Neigh to Necrophilia

In examining the chart that displays the different types of intimacies

    Emotional, spiritual, social, intellectual

We say Neigh to Necrophilia.

In pondering the mixture of elements on the 'chemie' diagram

    Chemise, chemistry, compatibility

We say Foo to Frotteurism.

In slicing and dicing all the words and exchanges

    Understanding, undemanding, lyrical gymnastics

We say Nada to Cuffs with chowder.

In dissecting the seven universal emotions, some more pertinent than others

Happiness, Sadness, Surprise

We reject bitter coffee with contempt.

In contemplating the road before us

Promise, justice, fidelity

We fuel each other with liberty.

Flowing with Fartlek along Lake Michigan

The first five minutes are so slow that it seems like a walk,
bouncing up and down with head so high that a
string lifts the cranium,
dispelling the ennui of a Monday morning.

The next ten minutes,
the shoes start to dance along the pavement of Water Street,
tiptoe, bruised toe,
improper thoughts, negligent thoughts, dreaming thoughts
cognition disappears as I enter the historic district.

My body craves the quickness of youth and I run like an infant
Speeding up and down the length of Water,
Two minutes of bullet train, slowing down to
Steam, my body enters the sauna of a hot summer morning.

Backwards and forwards between youth and age
The fast locomotive of Turner's Day, a technological innovation
Faster than hare or hounds,
returning to the shuffle of an old-fashioned passenger.

Flowing between, running between all the cracks on the road,
Peace in my body, chemical reduction, harmony within my form
My form of time and energy,
Returning to my place on the runner's second floor.

Leap into the Lake

The man has flippers for feet, he is
Grasping
The nylon bag that encloses the equipment
Ready for the triathlon.

The fog of summer grips his chest with a
Tugging
That reminds him of a time when he ate
Too much from too little love.

The runner, skinny and smart, watches the man
Descend into the waves of Lake stillness
Remembering a time when she consumed
Too many chocolate-covered confectionaries.

The man views the runner with peripheral vision
Closes his eyes, willing her to
Leap into the Lake with him
Exploring all the wonders of the sea, hand in hand.

Together, the pair explore all the treasures of the planet
The great Barrier Reef, the Caribbean shipwreck, lagoons
Chocked full of fish
The man blinks again and watches the runner disappear down the Lakefront path
A leap of faith into the turquoise pool of love and longing.

Looking Out from Lookout Mountain

In the dream, I am the wealthiest woman on the planet having inherited the house on Lookout Mountain.

My mother was the richest and kindest woman in the world. There was no gluttony or rivalry in the house, only gentleness and prosperity. In the dream, she has died and so I become heiress, my mouth aghast in shock and awe.

Because how can an imposter like me inherit all the wealth from an imaginary mother?

The kind of mother that authors dream about and write about. So flawless in thoughts and behavior that it seems unreal.

I awake from the dream and the history of Lookout Mountain is still in my thoughts.

Lookout Mountain so high in the sky, looking down on Chattanooga and all the tourists who float up the mountain on a railway tram, hoping to find the perfect view. Imagining the perfect family, the oasis, the perfect dream.

Lookout Mountain, whose history spans several lifetimes, and several states, Tennessee and Georgia fine. Men so rich that they could build mansions on top of the mountain and fight battles in the sky with the last men of the Cherokees. Stolen land so beautiful on the top of the mountain.

The stolen goods are passed down from generation to generation until the wealthy can claim it as their own.

When the rain pours down from the top of Lookout Mountain, the people in the valley below remember the tears that were shed.

Trails of tears as pockets of land were sold at the auction and purchased by men with the most money in their pockets, who became the elite of Tennessee.

The rain keeps pouring on the land and the tears turn to dust as the natives are forgotten and everything seems respectable in the valley.

I reflect on the legacy because my own mother died. Not the mother in the dream. A real-life mother who worked every day of her life to leave an inheritance for me.

A house in England near the Old Fort Hills, stolen from the Welsh several centuries before. Now respectable and a place where I lived. A memory of an imperfect place. Sometimes rich, sometimes poor.

Linking me to the southern state of Tennessee. To the place called Lookout Mountain.

Lily White

Snow-white Lily
You raise your sign high above the clouds
Looking outward towards the streets waiting
For the fanfare
Capturing hearts in minutes
Your sparkling smile to convey warmth, and sincerity
In your plea to save the planet
From the large Pacific garbage patch that is larger than England
Larger than France
You speak of community gardens, brimming with cabbage, pommes de terre, carrots
Without cares
Pleading to all that you care for the land from which you sprung
And those who you won gaze at you, in awe
Filling you up with sentiment, compliment, beneficence
This is what you need
Snow white Lily activist

Women of Afghanistan

Heads wrapped in azure, crystal blue, scarlet, sapphire

Eyes flashing with defiance as the soldiers stomp through the Kabul streets

The women show Iris, eyebrow, lid and lashes

To demand the keeping of rights.

In other places, the women run to the marketplace seeking burqas, to wrap

Around their faces, with prices so high ill can afford to feel the cloth against

Their skin, skin healthy from years without rule

The Taliban have reappeared, ready to seize all property.

The Taliban demand the woman cooks for them all of the

Delicious dishes they remember from childhood

Bolani stuffed full of mashed potato, lentils, leeks, scallions, pumpkin with

A Chakkah to add cream to the mouths of the men, the men

Who were once children.

Children, born into a technicolor nightmare where everything screeches so loud

That women are never forgotten, bound to their captors in the streets of Kabul, bound by family, lawlessness, power and control, haggled over, poured over,

Pounded for years until they resist, rising up like a Phoenix.

The women of Afghanistan take to the streets calling for participation, inclusion

In the upper corridors, waiting to be heard because without them

Society is a lifeless entity.

Toasty with Triage

Your fingers are wrapped around my back, as the fan swirls in the ceiling
Swirls of cold air zoom around the place to keep us cool as our
minds race
We are toasty in the covers as your mouth folds into mine.

I spot the grey in my toes as my legs curl around your broad back
Surprised at the strength in both of us as we stretch our limbs,
Curling and closing into each other, we are
Toasty with Triage.

The urgency to treat our wounds from the past subsides as our limbs
Discover the warmth from each other, terms of affection to each other,
Patient with each other, we kiss each other,
There is no need for a bandage.

You talk of a past time, I talk of mine, and you ask me to tell you how often:
I remember one time, the other time lodged deep inside my brain,
willing the memory
To erupt into present space.

It is only after you leave that the memory comes
Racing back to when he spoke of death in an instant,
Urgency of the need for treatment,
His body primed for pre-race action.

Free from the memory, my body wakes up to the aliveness in you
The triage from you, there is no need for a hospital bed or identification
The treatment came from your cool, slim fingers.

Away To Provence

There is something in the way that your hands sweep across my body
Conjuring an image of a place in Provence
The richness of your character captured by Cezanne in the
Consistent, reliable sweeps and swirls of the painter's brush
Depicting the Mountains in Provence

You touch me with the look of a wide-eyed child who has discovered the meaning
Of life, a life in the mountains away from all the bustle of the city and
You hold my hand like a boy, an innocent who has discovered the joy of being.

I close my eyes and we run together across the mountains and hills of France
The eagles soaring across the sky, the sparrows chirping to tell us that our
Life together is good, the best that nature can provide.

There is something in the way that your legs spring across the covers to
Remind me of a time when I ran across the mountains of North
Carolina
Singing as I drop down the hills to the valley, consuming pancakes, bacon,
Eggs and hash browns to fill up the emptiness inside.

You touch me with the peace that is found in the hills and streams of an
English countryside, the kind of land where children crave the taste of a
Crumpet, with dollops of butter melting into the bread, you
Remind me of my home.

You fire me up with a positive energy that makes me want to run to the
Shropshire Hills, just as splendid as Provence, and to clutch your hand
Exploring the twists in the country lanes and the English streams,
Jumping over stiles, laughing at the cows, and admiring the melancholy
Of the sheep, who beg for shearing.

By your side, we paint the canvas of a life together, with all the
possibilities of mountains, forests, lakes, and streams that cascade down
into our simple existence.
We travel together. We travel to Provence.

Pandemic Periodontal

Cookies or biscuits, the English Preference
One of the twenty-first century dilemmas
To eat or not to eat
Too many, too few
Some with chocolate, some with oats
Preference for white, dark, salted, or sprinkled with frosting
The dilemma for those with a sweet set of molars.

Cookies not an option for the periodontist table
To convey the importance of dental wash
Is the only brush with danger
The periodontist's family smiles so clean and bright
The periodontist never reveals the secrets
As her family takes a bite.

It is a pandemic periodontal brush
That maintains the gleaming smile
Wisdom teeth might vanish
As young succumb to the dentist's tools
The wish for life without dentures
Or the temptation of hardened sweets
The periodontist dilemma
To keep the nation's teeth.

Echo Ecstasy

Ewan elongated, ecstatic ease
Edinburgh Electric, eels squeal.
Every eejit, every Ethel, every Edna
Eats edibles, eats delectable, every easter.

Ecstasy elevates sense, smell, techno,
Ear erupts, eyes eek, Echo Ecstasy
Never Geek.

Ever Ecstasy, every teen
Feel effervescent
Be the queen.

Echo ecstasy
Pep, Pep
Pewk
Every teen
E-Bomb Eve

Elegy for living

And how will we live when our skin is as old as Dead Sea parchment and when
Our lips still touch with enthusiasm?

Without saying a word, the cabin in the center of a forest, replete with redwoods, crimson when the sun starts to glow above the cumulus, this is where
We dwell.

And what will you say when I tell you that you are sweet?
Will you deny it, as is your way, or indulge in the words as I show you
The evidence of how you have touched others who broke into too many pieces
With your strong hands, weathered by oak.

And how will you feel when I whisper into your ear?
My love for you is rich and has depth like the thickness of plums, ripened
Darkness with Light.

And how will I surrender when you sweep me into your arms, browned by the sun
So yellow in the blue sky, it blinds us for a moment, as our arms circle around each other
So close, it is hard to see the divide between us, as we get closer and closer
To Unity.

And when will we weep?
It seems so impossible to weep and to yearn because the magic of being together is so exquisite, like raindrops falling on parched ash trees
The tears when they come will be a long-ago memory, wedged inside our minds, like a book nestled inside a case, the tears will come like a storm.

And for whom will we pray when locked inside each other at night when the whole world is asleep?
Together we pray for those on the margins, invisible, forgotten, scorned like the fruit,
Too ripe for eating and too old for fermenting, we pray for them all
Together we hold.

Take You Home

I take you inside my heart across the pond to the home of childhood
Placing you upon my favorite chair
We toss another coal on the fire
The poker prods the coal and the embers inside my heart
Tell me you are with me in the home
Where I once lived.

You listen to the accents of Salopian, English, Welsh, Irish, and European
I wait for the sound of your voice, as quiet as the mist that unfurls
And twists around the willow, chestnut, oak, and apple.

Inside the kitchen, the stove is modern, complete with electric circles
The only difference is the smallness of the rooms
Small enough to fit into one American Studio
You fit into my home with your humility.

At night, across the pond, we climb into my childhood bed
A single size, so small, we curl into spoons, tight
Like a child ready for love inside the home of play.

In the morning, we wake to the chill of winter
The kind of cold to dampen the joints and you
Rub my fingers to remind me that you are in my home.

In my home, I cradle your heart in my hands, so soft and luxurious
Like the velvet that we wore as schoolgirls, a multiplicity of colors
To represent each of our school homes.

Inside the kitchen, we cook over the stove, hot porridge, thick
With sugar and raisins, picking up spoons
To feed each other, touching each other's faces
To remind us of the comfort of home.

Marathon Blues

For those who cross the finish line with personal bests or the goal to claim a medal, there are those
Who do not start: There are those who do not finish.

For those who do not finish, there is a logical explanation: the knee that flares up at mile sixteen, the lack of desire to complete the distance, the lack of training, the voice of Monsieur Lucifer who whispers in your ear at Mile 22: A plausible reason for not finishing.

And what of those who do not start?
A myriad of possibilities. Those who trained and were injured, not making it to the starting line. Those who slept too late and missed the bus, and those who thought of other more pleasant things to do.

All are winners because they started something and what of those who never start?
Whose complexities and societal demands force a struggle with the body through chemicals, a shot in the arm, injections to make the brain do somersaults, the pleasure of the pipe and the trips through the outer planets only to land face-first: not during the marathon, during the passage of a life.

And what of those who run the marathon in memory of a lost one? The father who just gasped his last breath, the son whose car wheels screeched before rolling over, and the daughter of the Cherokee Tribe who went missing. Where are their memories on the marathon route?

They are embedded in every step of the marathoners, every bead of sweat, every gasp for air, every limp, every mile, every station, every smile, every tear.

The marathoners skip and race down the road to the lakeshore, gazing up at the clouds and the birds that fly through the sky, remembering those who have gone, and those who remain at home.
The marathoners, grateful to be alive.

The Difficult Ones

In compiling a list of those to avoid, there are the obvious suspects.
It is not a long list merely composed of those who drag you down to the depths of hell, those who cringe at the sight of soft gel, and those who don't get any.

They are labeled The Difficult Ones.

There is the office worker who has never gone out to lunch and the retired fireman
Who occasionally remembers he has a son, and those who don't have any children. The ones who cry in the night.

The difficult ones receive a badge that says Remedial, at best, longing
For the excellence badge, given to those with zest.

The difficult ones listen to the murmurs of the popular ones, wondering how it feels
To have the whole world on their knees, just the slightest blink bringing grown men to tears at the very sight of the beloved faces of the homegrown rock stars.

The difficult ones gain attention for a few moments when they trip on something walking up the stairs, just for a moment their five minutes of fame reduced to a thirty second Instagram video.

In a moment it is gone, fame and fortune slipping out of their grasp as they contemplate their mere existence on the planet, wondering if it is ever worth bothering to get up in
The morning to see the sun rise, blood red at night, pondering their lack of recognition in the amplified zoom of everyday life.

Kiss For a Therapist

Because you are my client we are not allowed to kiss, so I gaze at you like you are the most wonderful person in the whole wide world, trauma ripped from your limbic system, lyrical in your emotions, musical in your melancholia, you howl on the couch, the incidents of shaming and blaming screech like sirens on the shore and run from your body, your body that has held them for so long.
Because you are my client we are not allowed to touch, my gaze falls on you in admiration of the fight that you experienced, wishing you, wanting you to perceive yourself as the most wonderful soul in the world, your thoughts stomp through your mind, defining you, refining you, so I look at you like a mother looks at her new-born baby.
Long after the session is over, and your howling has ceased, I return home to the man that I love, who gives me a kiss to ease the rip in my chest, because the session reminded me of a time that someone screamed at me with all the bite of the banshees' cry.

Kisses from my partner to Me and there are so many kisses to heal the rip in my chest: Kisses that are long and lingering in the linen and the passion that comes from my beloved's hold: and a kiss that comes in the quietness of two souls, a gentle kiss
on my forehead to remind me that I was once a lost child and a soft kiss to tell me that I am so bold.

Education For Americans

In England, the posh people use the word Twaddle or Codswallop
The working class prefer the sound of Rubbish or Crap.

In England, the upper class have separate bedrooms with no discussion
The working class talk about it a lot and Saturday night turns into Hangover Sunday.

In jolly England, the humor is of the dry and sarcastic kind with little time for slapstick
With humor of the erotic kind, the English prefer to call it smut.

Before the dawn of Thatcher, Margaret not the occupation, and there were two groups:
Upper and lower, that is all, nothing more, nothing less between the socioeconomic status and the English know their place.

After the Thatcher reign of terror, there were three groups:
Upper, lower and those in between who turned quite nasty when Mrs. Jones had a pond installed in her back garden.

In England, there are several kinds of curry to eat and a favorite of the English is the Chicken Vindaloo
Fish and Chips come a close second with roast dinners at the top of the pack.

Before the Internet, the typical British family sat down on a Sunday to curse and complain about the weather while tucking into a big meal: Roast Beef, Yorkshire Pudding, Brussel Sprouts, Roast Potatoes, and very thick gravy with horseradish or Mustard on the side.

The English find Americans glamorous and wonder how it feels to be a Hollywood film star, the English like the Queen.

On the subject of dating in England, the upper class mingle with their own, the middle class enjoy a glass of wine with a kiss under the mistletoe
The working class like to snog.

If invited to a wedding in England, the upper class know everyone, the middle class envy the superior wedding cake
The working class look for some other.

In England there are various interpretations of the word 'crumpet'
For some, it is delicious bread with small holes smeared with the delight of a thick knob of butter
For others it is used in the phrase 'smashing bit of crumpet' and is the American equivalent of hot.

In England, people go to church and scoff at the notion of religion
The English choose to wear their best outfits commonly referred to as Sunday best
Followed by a trip to the pub and a return home to Lamb, peas, potatoes, and mint sauce with gravy.

Among the English Upper classes, it is proper to say pardon
Among the middle classes, it is polite for the English to apologize and say I am sorry
When the English use the phrase 'excuse me' it is considered an insult flavored with sarcasm.

The English say rubber to describe an eraser and the English will laugh when they hear the phrase 'fanny pack'
Such is the humor of the common English person.
Such is the delight of being Upper, middle, or working English class.

A picture of us

My face next to your neck
Gentle coo from my lips to your skin
Lightly tanned from your runs around Lake Park
I smell your stubble
Facial hair to frame your face
So genial
I want to parler Francais with you

My dress peaks into the picture
A dress first worn with the price tag
Still attached to the back
Light blue to compliment
Your deep brown eyes of soul

The soul within you stretches
Across the picture
Your eyes look deep into my soul
Binding us together
Into the camera lens
The secrets that we hold
Your perfect features
Nose, brows, eyes,
Spectacles round

Gaze at me without opinion
Skin so smooth
Your humble mouth

Tentatively, I look at the camera
Teeth white with flecks
Pearl earring to compliment
The white button on your shirt

Both our necks tilt towards the lens
Our throats like
Flutes filled with the finest white wine
Our eyes sparkle like sprinkles of rain

Your arm
Wrapped around my shoulders
Like a warm scarf
To keep the cold out in the air-conditioned room

Your touch
On my arm
To remind the camera
Who we are.

About the Author

Annette Towler was born in England and moved to the United States in the early 1990s. She enjoys her job as a therapist and in her spare time she like to run. Annette has a sweet cat called Marsha.